Inside You'll Discover How To Get On Google's 1st Page of Search...

Skyrocket Your Local Business Sales With <u>FREE</u> Online Advertising...

Get More Customers & Clients Today!

Search Engine Success for Newbies
by K. Hill

Copyright ©2011 by K. Hill
All rights reserved. This book or any portion thereof
may not be reproduced or used in any manner whatsoever
without the express written permission of the publisher
except for the use of brief quotations in a book review.

Printed in the United States of America

First Printing, 2011

ISBN-13: 978-1466491861
ISBN-10: 1466491868

Eclectic Design Studio
7601 W. 185th Street
Tinley Park, IL 60477

www.EclecticDesignStudio.net

TABLE OF CONTENTS

I'm Too Busy Running My Business To Think About All Of This 'Internet Stuff' **9**

Crafting A Powerful USP **12**

Laser-Targeted Lead Generation **20**

The Yellow Pages Is Dead **24**

What Is SEO? **29**

Fishing With the Right Bait: Keyword Research **30**

'Show Me The Money' Keywords **34**

Maximizing Your Key(word) Moneymaker **35**

Google Related Search **37**

Ringing The Register With Google AdWords **40**

The Power Of Google Places **41**

Optimizing Your Images **44**

Online Directories **45**

Using Article Directories And Press Releases To Increase Search Rankings **48**

Promoting Your Product With Online Video **50**

Google Trends **56**

How To Avoid Online Overwhelm **57**

Internet Terms Decoded **61**

I'm Too Busy Running My Business To Think About All Of This 'Internet Stuff'

You are probably reading this book because you understand the power of website traffic and the potential benefits it has to bring free advertising and online exposure to your business. But did you know that the top four results from a Google search or any other search engines, get over seventy percent of the clicks? Yes, over seventy percent! If you are the 5th thru 8th link on the search results page, the percentage of clicks you will receive drops down to approximately two or three percent. If you're on the second page of Google, your website may never get clicked on at all. It is a harsh reality for today's business competing for sales.

Yet by increasing your search engine rankings, you create more awareness about your brand, your product, your website, or your business blog. And while optimizing an online presence for higher search engine rankings is not complicated stuff, to be quite honest, it can be a time-consuming endeavor.

As far as optimization goes, the work that you do on your website to optimize it for higher search rankings is perhaps only a fraction of your online popularity, so to speak. Some estimates state only twenty percent of your online optimization accounts for your website's popularity (i.e. how often and how high you show up in search engine results). The remaining eighty percent of your website optimization comes from what happens off of your site. What keyword phrases other sites are using when they link to your site. What happens on Facebook, what is being tweeted on Twitter, what is covered in the press when articles are written about you or your company, what is happening in your Google + circles of influence, etc. In essence, the sum total of the online conversation going on about you and/or business.

Search Engine Optimization, otherwise known as SEO, are the tactics used to target traffic to a website through natural search (a.k.a. organic) results as opposed to paid search (a.k.a. Pay-per-click). Again, research shows that the first four listings of organic search results get an overwhelming 70% of the clicks. That is why it's crucial to get on page one for your targeted keywords.

The good news is that by harnessing the power of the internet and wireless communications, you can compete with the big dogs without the overhead expenses and corporate bureaucracy inherent with big box corporations. That is great news for home-based and small business owners!

Essentially, you are creating multiple opportunities to get in front of your potential customers at precisely the time they are ready to buy. As a result you'll enjoy the benefits that come along with generating substantial income and the lifestyle freedom of generating that income on your own terms.

As long as you provide value to your customer base and keep their needs in the forefront, you will continue to be rewarded with on-going business and referrals.

What does it really take to have a website that is profitable?

1) **Getting traffic** – It's important to get ranked for terms that are targeted to your business and have a high monthly search volume.

2) **Capturing leads** – You need to offer something of value for free on your website in exchange for collecting your visitor's phone number and/or email address. Nine times out of ten a visitor will not buy from you on their very first visit. Capturing their name and email offers you the opportunity to start building a relationship and market to them over time.

3) **Start building a relationship** – Now that you have your prospects contact information, send them useful information that sells them on doing business with you. You can do this automatically with your 'silent salesperson' also known as an Auto-responder.

4) **Following up with your leads** – By tapping into Twitter, Facebook, LinkedIn and YouTube, you can start building relationships with your prospects and customers that is lasting and benefits you both.

In order for your local business to get good rankings in local search results, you're going to need local keyword phrases on your website and in your blog content. For example, if your company sells carpet cleaning services, then it is ideal for your homepage to feature content that specifies the various 'carpet cleaning' services that you offer such as rug cleaning, pet odor removal, mattress cleaning and water damage restoration. However, don't stop at merely listing your services on your website, include helpful articles, tips and videos that discuss theses particular services. As you do so, you will naturally make your website keyword rich and thus improve your search engine rankings for those targeted keywords specific to your industry.

By now, you have developed your company's website and are using it as a marketing tool on auto-pilot, providing valuable information to potential customers twenty-four hours a day, seven days a week, totally at their convenience. You've also incorporated compelling calls-to-action that encourage visitors to either join your email list or make a purchase. Right now you may be thinking, 'isn't that enough?'

Google is the number one most visited site on the internet, so it makes sense that we will focus most of our attention there. But understand that the strategies we will cover are effective across all of the major search engines. Yahoo, Bing, Ask and other search engines also pick up on these keyword search strategies, so you will gain even more effectiveness and reach when you expand to those networks as well.

You can have the greatest product in the world, but if you have no sales, then you have no business and will quickly be forced to close your doors. In order to get sales, you have to spread the word about the value of your product or service and compel people to take action. And that's where marketing comes into play.

People who are local (i.e. in your geographic area) are looking for a location, as opposed to information. They know exactly what they want but they just don't know a place nearby to go and get it. For you to reach this crowd and get results that translate into sales, you need to use search terms that include both your city, your neighborhood and zip code for a boost in "search engine juice," placing your business in the local spotlight. We will uncover the search terms so critical to your online success, also known as keywords, in later chapters. But first we must lay the foundation by identifying the position you hold in the marketplace.

Crafting A Powerful USP

To put it simply, a USP is your **'unique selling proposition,'** a strong benefit statement that quickly and succinctly describes the most compelling reason why someone should buy from you. It is what distinguishes you from your target audience and lets them know how and in what way they will benefit by doing business with you.

It is a key cornerstone to the effective advertising & marketing of your business, both online and offline. Your unique selling proposition pinpoints what it is that makes your business unique. It answers that main question: "Why should I buy from you as opposed to any and all other options available to me? Including doing nothing."

Developing a USP takes a bit of reflective thought so this book includes a worksheet that will guide you through the thought process. First you will list the three main products or services you offer. Second, you will describe what problem your product or service solves. Think in terms of what your target markets' pain points are. What is keeping them up at night? What problems are they desperately trying to solve? Essentially, you want to uncover what your prospects' needs are and how your product or service meets those needs.

When thinking about how your product or service addresses the problems your target prospect is desperately trying to solve, also think about how do your competitors' products address this problem? Again, why should a customer buy from you as opposed to anyone else?

By answering the following questions, you will be able to identify the unique selling proposition of your business and subsequently convey that benefit in all of your marketing efforts. (Feel free to use extra paper if you run out of space.)

1. **List the three main products or services you offer:**

   _____
   _____
   _____
   _____
   _____

2. **List the top three problems that your product or service solves:**

   _____
   _____
   _____
   _____
   _____
   _____
   _____

3. **Describe the pain points of your target market? What keeps them up at night? What problems are they desperately trying to solve? Even if your product or service does not offer them.**

   _____
   _____
   _____
   _____
   _____
   _____

4. **Referring to Question #3, which solution(s) do you provide?**

   _____
   _____
   _____
   _____
   _____
   _____

5. **How do your solutions compare to your competitors?**

   _____
   _____
   _____

What's Your Elevator Pitch?

Are you familiar with the phrase 'elevator pitch?' Basically, an elevator pitch is the ability to sum up your business and describe it to others in a way that excites them and inspires them to want to know more about you, your product or service. An elevator pitch is short and to the point, based on the idea that if you got into the elevator on the first floor with your dream client or investor, you would have until reaching the tenth floor to tell them about your business so that they understand it and could explain it to someone else. It would also engage their interest enough to want to know more about your business.

An elevator pitch must be described in thirty seconds (or two to three sentences) and ideally captivates the listener as well. It's something you will practice over and over until it rolls off your tongue at dinner parties and networking events.

You are likely to hear terms like branding, marketing, advertising, elevator pitch and USP tossed around various business circles and industry conferences. But it is important to note the differences. Especially between branding and marketing. Every year, big companies spend millions on building their brand. A brand holds equity in the mental real estate of your potential clients and customers. So it is important to think about brand building as you are building your business. But as a small business owner, it is much more important to market your business because marketing is what brings sales in the front door. And when done properly, your brand is built as an extension of your marketing efforts.

According to About.com — "your brand resides within the hearts and minds of customers; clients and prospects. It is the sum total of their experiences and perceptions, some of which you can influence, and some that you cannot."

Remember, it is not about you...it is all about your prospect or customer. How can you position yourself as different from your competitors in their eyes? Because, if you are not different, you are a commodity and commodities compete on price. Walmart is the perfect example of this.

Let us look at toothpaste as another example. Is there much difference in a customers mind between Crest, Colgate and Aquafresh? They all have anti-cavity, fluoride, tartar control and whitening properties, right? So when you are in the grocery store aisle and about to make a selection, what is the differentiator? You've guessed it...whatever is on sale. BUT, what if Arm & Hammer or Tom's of Maine toothpaste is now added to your choice of options? Now you have the choice of a toothpaste with baking soda built into it and a toothpaste that is 'all natural' so depending on where your values and priorities lie, that will determine your selection and then it really doesn't matter what the cost is as compared to the other options.

So what is *your company's* differentiator?

Another way to differentiate yourself is to have a story. Does your company have a story? How can you use your company's story to generate interest or be memorable? What are the values and goals of your company and how can you communicate them through your daily conducting of business?

For example, Patagonia is an outdoor apparel company that is deeply committed to environmental issues and sustainability. They have been committed to this far before it ever became popular or trendy to be a 'green' business. Having a passion drives their business decisions and also gives customers an added incentive to do business with them. A customer feels confident that in some small way, by making a purchase, they are putting their dollars towards reducing their carbon footprint and helping the environment. This can go a long way in building brand equity, encouraging repeat sales and creating an army of volunteer brand ambassadors.

So when we think in terms of our target audience, who exactly are we talking to?

It is extremely dangerous to make broad generalizations like 'my product is for men and women ages 25-55.' The people that fall in this category run the gamut in terms of interests, hobbies, biases and preferences. There is no way your marketing piece will speak to such a large group of people, and nowadays, you have to speak to the individual in order to break through the clutter of all of the marketing messages they are bombarded with everyday. Consumer Reports website estimates that the average American is exposed to 247 commercial messages each day. The Business Journal of Phoenix places that estimate at closer to 600. That is an awful lot of NOISE.

Therefore, you want to know exactly who you're speaking to in order to market to them effectively.

One way to do this is to simply ask yourself, what type of customer do you want to do business with?

Create an actual persona for them...

What does your ideal customer look like? Who are they?

Describe them...

Give them a real name.

How old are they? Are they married? Do they have kids? Are they male or female?

What do they do for a living? How much do they make? Where do they work? What kind of neighborhood do they live in?

For example, if they make a good living then you might emphasize quality in your marketing efforts, whereas if they are pinching every dollar, you could emphasize bargain values instead of stressing quality.

What do they like to do for fun and recreation? Do they have any hobbies? Describe them.

What do they believe in?

Do they belong to any community groups?

'Hey, You're Talking To Me!'

Your marketing materials are more effective when they speak to a specific person. The goal is to get your ideal prospect to see your marketing piece, read it and say *'hey, that's me!'* which causes them to recognize you as talking specifically to them.

You can use your USP to speak to and reach your ideal customer through your brand identity, including your logo, flyers, etc... all of your marketing and advertising.These materials essentially become laser-focused marketing tools that prescreens prospects for you. You can then spend less time qualifying a prospect and more time closing the sale.

If you don't know who your target audience is, start by asking your current customers. Ask your customers in person or use a brief, informal questionnaire, solicit their feedback and get testimonials that you will repurpose throughout your marketing materials.

One easy way to get feedback is with online surveys like PollDaddy.com or SurveyMonkey.com. They are free for you and convenient for your customers and clients to complete.

By knowing exactly who your target audience is, you will have more confidence when communicating with them and connecting with them more effectively.

Some additional key information you can gather from your target audience include:

- Are they businesses or consumers?
- What do they think about your current brand?
- How will you attract them to your product or service?
- Who else is competing for their loyalty and devotion?
- What type of relationship would you like to have with them?
- How often would you like to see them or do business with them?

Jay Conrad Levinson, marketing legend and the author of the book, Guerilla Marketing says this...

"Focus on markets and target audiences vs. trying to be all things to mass markets."

Laser-Targeted Lead Generation

The reason it is important to know your USP (unique selling proposition) and to first identify your target market before diving into an online marketing strategy is because by laser-targeting who you are talking to and what you want to tell them (by understanding what they desperately want to know) you don't have to waste any more money blindly pushing out your message to those who may not even be interested. This makes your lead-generation very productive. When you are deciding on your lead-generation strategy, here are a few things to consider to make it the most effective:

1) **Offer something for free** – This is a key step. Whether you are doing direct mail, blogging, Craigslist ads, print media or television, you should offer something for free to get your prospect to raise his/her hand to say, 'I'm interested, tell me more.' Some ideas for free offers include a free report, free gift, free analysis, free inspection, free catalog, free consultation or pretty much anything your target audience considers valuable and is related to your product or service.

2) **Hit your prospects pain point** – Help them solve a problem. You'll definitely get and hold their attention. For example, for someone with painful corns and callouses, offering a 'free booklet on eliminating corns in 24 hours' is much more appealing than a free booklet about XYZ Foot Care Center.

3) **Keep It Simple** – Don't get carried away with flashy graphics and animated banners, make sure that the message is clear, generates interest and includes a call to action to yield some type of response. Ugly design actually has its place in generating response when used purposefully.

4) **Follow up fast** – A hot lead cools off much more quickly now that we have gotten so accustomed to receiving instant feedback which includes overnight delivery, instant text messaging, live chat on customer service websites and so forth. Always make sure your contact forms are working, your listed telephone numbers are up to date and follow up on all inquiries within 24-48 hours (within the same working day if possible). Otherwise, clearly state your business or customer service hours on your website so that customers know what to expect.

Everyday, consumers are using the internet to make buying decisions. As a local business owner, you have to create multiple opportunities to get in front of them online at precisely the time they are ready to buy. If you neglect this, your competitors will be there and the sale will go to them.

Let us look at one example in particular, back in April the idea of celebrating Customer Loyalty month came to mind. A direct mail promotion would be used as way to show appreciation to the loyal clients who utilized my marketing & design services over the course of the past twelve months. Thus, sending "gratitude cookies" to all of my past clients, thanking them for their business seemed like an appropriate gesture. Decorative cookies in a shape that could be tied into the promotional theme was also important. So what did I do? I went online and did a Google search for "custom cookies 60430" which resulted in listing all of the nearby bakeries in my area that offered custom cookies.

Now at this moment in time, I have no point of reference or preference for any of these places. One local bakery is just as good as another. So I click on the bakeries that have a website. Ones without a website automatically get disqualified because I'm not going to waste time traveling to their location only to discover they don't have what I'm looking for. I scan the websites for a bakery that can create custom shaped cookies for me and 'voila' I end up at Sweet Annie's Everyday Treats in downtown Flossmoor. And another sale is made. That is the power of online marketing for your small business. Now just imagine if you are creating opportunities like that for your business around the clock, even while you sleep. How powerful is that?

Now let us transition into the actual execution of maximizing your online marketing. It is time to create an advertisement and let the world know you are open and ready to serve them.

Creating A Cohesive Image

The American Marketing Association (AMA) defines a brand as a "name, term, design, symbol, or any other feature that identifies one seller's good or service as distinct from those of other sellers."

A strong brand is invaluable and serves as the visual equivalent of your promise to your consumer. Although you can help shape your brand by taking the lead in its formation and presentation to the marketplace, you cannot control how it takes hold of the marketplace. Your brand ultimately resides within the hearts and minds of your customers, clients, and probable purchasers. It's the sum total of *their* experiences and perceptions, which you can influence but you cannot control.

It takes far more money to establish your company's brand than it does to market your company's products and services. In addition, you cannot see a tangible and immediate return on your branding efforts (i.e. more sales) as compared to your marketing efforts. Therefore, it is a smarter choice for small business owners like yourself to focus attention on marketing your products and services and let the branding result as an extension of your marketing efforts.

All of your marketing materials, your logo, business card, website, postcards, etc., should communicate a streamlined message that attracts your target audience to you like a magnet. It also is intended to create confidence in your brand while differentiating you from any of your competitors. So keep these materials consistent throughout your marketing efforts.

Are you tired of spending marketing and advertising dollars without any way to track its impact, effectiveness, or return on investment?

Are you guilty of cutting back on advertising dollars spent because of poor response?

Well, since we know that you have to continually promote your services in order to generate new and repeat business, one very effective way to solve this dilemma is to start implementing a direct response approach in all of your marketing efforts from this day forward. This means that whenever you send out a piece or promotion, or do anything online it will have a method for garnering some type of response from your target prospect.

The Yellow Pages Is Dead

Many marketing experts will argue that the Yellow Pages is dead, and for some categories we can all agree that it is no longer very effective, especially with the use of online searches and smartphone apps. Quite frankly, in most cases, it is much easier, and a heck of a lot faster to hop on your phone or computer, type your search and receive instant results rather than to go to the back of the closet, dig out the Yellow Pages book, thumb through the categories and search for a listing.

But I digress, let's think of how a typical Yellow Pages ad is laid out. Normally, it features a big bold company name or logo with contact information. It may include a list of services or a picture of the company vehicle, but usually not much more than that. When you have ten to twenty of those type of ads on a page, what is going to make any one of them stand out? What is going to compel you to pick up the phone and dial one of those numbers?

Truth is, not much...

Regular ads typically focus on the razzle-dazzle of bold color and pretty pictures to help their ads stand out. But when someone is looking for a solution to an immediate problem, which is why your prospect is thumbing through the Yellow Pages in the first place, a bright color is not going to help them make an informed decision about which service provider to select. Regular ads are awareness builders at best.

But as a smart marketer of your local business, what you want is to get them to pick up the phone and call *you*. So how do you do that?

By including a clear Call-To-Action.

K.I.S.S. Method To Getting The Sale

Tell them exactly what you want them to do next.

Is it call a telephone number? If so, give them a compelling reason why. Perhaps, give them a free report, free recorded message of useful and timely information (remember to hit the pain point), or schedule a free estimate.

If it is a printed piece, you can direct them to your website or mail a response card to request additional information that they will find useful. By doing this, you capture the home advantage in getting that initial contact, offering to solve their problem and win their business. This also provides you with the golden nugget of marketing which is the prospects contact information. Now you can follow-up and continue to market to them over time, becoming top of mind whenever they are ready to buy.

Wikipedia describes Direct Response marketing as a form of marketing designed to solicit a direct response which is specific and measurable. The delivery of the response is directly between the viewer and the advertiser. That is, the customer responds to the marketer directly, as opposed to doing so through a middleman such as a retailer or distribution center.

So from now on, the primary objectives of your marketing efforts will be to:

- Deliver a clear and succinct message
- Confirm your credibility in the prospect's mind
- Connect with your target prospects on an emotional level
- Motivate them to take a specific action. You will do this simply by telling them what action you want them to take
- And lastly to further solidify customer loyalty by demonstrating value.

Quick question for you...

What is your favorite radio station? I would bet that everyone who is reads this book shares the same favorite station.

And it's called Wii-FM — **What's In It For Me?**

Everyone, no matter how altruistic, is concerned primarily with him or herself. So when speaking to your potential customers and clients, you will get far better results by focusing on their concerns and placing them first and foremost in your marketing efforts.

The first course of action you can take is to identify all of the bullet points in your marketing messages and on your website that refer to "we" and "our" and replace them with points that focus on "you" and "your."

There is a great article in Inc magazine written by Jason Fried of 37signals, a popular web apps development company, who talks about the banality of boring business writing. I would encourage you to read the full article online at your earliest opportunity.

In the article he writes...

> *"One of my favorite phrases in the business world is 'full-service solutions provider.' A quick search on Google finds at least 47,000 companies using that one. That's full-service generic. There is more. 'Cost effective end-to-end solutions' brings you about 95,000 results. 'Provider of value-added services' nets you more than 600,000 matches. Exactly which services are sold as not adding value?*
>
> *Who writes this stuff? Worse, who reads it and approves it? What does it say when tens of thousands of companies are saying the same things about themselves?*

When you write like everyone else and sound like everyone else and act like everyone else, you are saying, "Our products are like everyone else's, too." Or think of it this way: Would you go to a dinner party and just repeat what the person to the right of you is saying all night long? Would that be interesting to anybody? So why are so many businesses saying the same things at the biggest party on the planet -- the marketplace?"

Keep in mind that the people who read marketing messages are most interested in **BENEFITS NOT FEATURES.**

Benefits are things like:

- ☑ saving time
- ☑ saving money
- ☑ highest quality (but be specific, state how)
- ☑ feeling empowered

Here is an example of how a tanning salon can translate their features into a benefit for the customer:

Feature: The number of tanning beds or manicure stations a salon has.

Benefit: The beautiful golden tan you will receive or how your nail polish will last a full two weeks!

So when you are developing the content for your "About Us" page or your "Services We Offer" page, keep your benefits versus features in mind. Your potential customer does not care to hear about how great you already are, they want to hear how great you will make them look, feel or become!

The internet is clearly a 24/7 platform for constant connectivity...

But did you know that eighty-three percent of local search users search for a business online and then contact that business offline?

What this is saying to us is that new media marketing needs to be a part of your marketing mix for maximum exposure and leverage of your marketing and advertising dollars. But with new media tools sprouting up like wildfire everyday, how can you use them effectively to grow your business without becoming overwhelmed and scattered?

Wii-FM

Keeping Wii-FM in mind will help direct your online marketing efforts and identify which ones will give you the most return for your time, luckily this route is less costly than traditional advertising. However, the trade-off is time...it is more time-consuming to execute.

The goal with email marketing, social media marketing and most all of the new media marketing strategies is to develop a relationship with your potential customer.

If you think you have no time for social media, find a student, work-at-home parent or use your office assistant. It is critical to your business success in the new economy.

What Is SEO?

Search engine optimization (SEO) is the process of improving the visibility of a website or a web page in search engines via the "natural" or un-paid ("organic" or "algorithmic") search results. Other forms of search engine marketing (SEM) target paid listings. In general, the earlier or higher on the page, and more frequently a site appears in the search results list, the more visitors it will receive from the search engine's users. SEO may target different kinds of search, including image search, local search, video search and industry-specific vertical search engines. This gives a website its web presence.

As an internet marketing strategy, SEO considers how search engines work, what people search for, the actual search terms typed into search engines and which search engines are preferred by their targeted audience.

Optimizing a website may involve editing its content and HTML and associated coding to both increase its relevance to specific keywords and to remove barriers to the indexing activities of search engines. Promoting a site to increase the number of back-links, or inbound links, is another SEO tactic.

Fishing With the Right Bait: Keyword Research

Coming up with a master keyword list is an essential first step in making your website rank higher in the search engines. The more relevant your pages are, the more the search engines will favor them and serve the content up to its users. The more competitive the keyword is, the harder it will be to rank for it (example: dog food). But if you can develop what is called long-tail keywords, then you have a greater chance as a local business to rank on the first page for your keywords (example: best dog food for white terriers)

Keyword research is a process of uncovering the critical buying terms that fit your site and your audience, then directing each term to a specific page of your site.

This part of the SEO equation is very important because if your site is targeting the wrong keywords, the search engines and your customers may never find you, or worse yet, end in frustration when they do, resulting in lost dollars and rankings that do not make you money. If you spend time targeting the wrong keywords, you waste valuable advertising dollars and throw away all the time and energy you put into getting your site to rank for those terms in the first place.

One of the strongest barriers to overcome in your keyword research for a search engine optimization campaign is the assumption that you already know which terms a customer would use to find your site. You do not. Not without first doing some research. You may know what your site is about and how you, the site owner, would find it, but that is not to say that a paying customer would go about looking for it in the same way. It is best not to guess when a little research will provide the answers.

When describing your site's product or service, resist the urge to use industry jargon. Your customers are not searching that way and if you focus your site on these terms, they will never find you. Being ranked number one for a term no one would associate with your product or service is both a waste of time and money. Sure, your site may see a lot of traffic, but customers won't stick around. And they certainly won't buy.

So let's get started creating our list of potential keywords. Brainstorm all the words you think a customer would type into their search box when trying to find you. For now this includes thinking of phrases that are quite broad but also very specific, buying and information-gathering terms, and single words and long-tail phrases. What is your site hoping to do or promote? Come up with enough words to cover all the terms related to the services your site offers. Avoid overly generic terms like 'shirts' or 'hats.' These words are nearly impossible to rank for and what's more, they don't deliver qualified traffic to your site. Focus on words that are relevant, but not rendered useless by overexposure.

Next we will determine the activity for each of your proposed keywords. You want to narrow your list to only include highly attainable, sought-after phrases that will bring the most qualified traffic to your site. Fortunately there are lots of great tools out there to help you uncover how much activity your keywords are receiving:

Google AdWords Keyword Tool: The Keyword Tool lets you look up popular keyword phrases to determine their activity and popularity among competitors. You can find the terms that are most frequently searched for, or compare the competitiveness of each phrase. This is very useful for figuring out how difficult it will be to rank for a given term. It may also reveal hidden gems that have low competition-rates, but are highly relevant to your target market.

Google Suggest: Google Suggest is a great way to find synonyms and related word suggestions that may help you expand your original list. Just start typing your search term and you'll see a drop down list of related terms appear provided the Google suggest feature is turned on in your web browser.

Thesaurus.com: Use this to identify additional synonyms you may have overlooked.

Understanding the competition tells you how much effort you will need to invest in order to rank well for that term. There are two things to pay attention to when making this decision: how many other sites are competing for the same word or phrase and how strong those sites' rankings are (i.e. how many other sites link to them, how many pages do they have indexed)? Basically, is that word or phrase even worth your time? If it is too competitive then perhaps move on and pick another word or phrase to target.

For example, say your company sells cowboy boots. Initially you may think it is a natural fit to focus on the terms "boots" and "cowboy boots." These words are important because they tell the search engines what you do and may increase your visitors, but the traffic you receive will be largely unqualified. Customers will arrive on your site still unsure of what kind of boots you sell. Do you offer traditional cowboy boots, ostrich boots, suede cowboy boots or men's cowboy boots? If you only target broad terms, customers won't know what you offer until they land on your site.

Targeted terms and long-tail keyword phrases are easier to rank for and direct qualified traffic to your site. Targeted, buying-oriented terms like these maximize conversions meaning the people that type in such specific phrases are ready to buy something *right now*.

Be sure to also incorporate the keywords into the content on your website and steer clear of over-repetition which can be considered spamming. Your content should never sound forced.

To further maximize search engine rankings, keywords could also be used in several other elements on your site:

- Title Tags
- Meta Description Tags
- Headings
- Alt text
- Anchor Text/ Navigational Links

Getting first page search engine placement is the offline equivalent of choosing your store's physical location in a high traffic metropolitan area. You know what they say...*location is everything.* You want to be in high traffic areas where your target audience is most likely to find you, not tucked in some back alley where the only foot traffic you see is the occasional dumpster diver with no money to spend.

Keyword research is the foundation of all your online marketing efforts. All too often a business owner chooses their keywords on one or two factors: search volume, and/or what a competitor is doing. This is good information to have, but neither should be a sole reason to pick a keyword to try and aggressively rank for. While it is a good idea to analyze your competition to see what keywords they are targeting as part of their SEO efforts, you don't want to automatically use a phrase or keyword that they used, just because *they* used it. You do not know how effective their keyword strategy is or whether that keyword increases sales or generates leads for your competitor.

Remember, by removing the guesswork in developing your keyword campaigns, you no longer have to waste precious advertising dollars on keywords that don't perform because no one is using those keywords to find the information they are looking for related to your product or service.

'Show Me The Money' Keywords

Pick your brain and make a list of all the keywords related to your business. What is important when you are brainstorming your keywords is to think like a customer.

For example, a doctor might search for "hallux valgus" whereas a customer is going to search for "bunion." You may think "podiatrist" is a good keyword to target, but in actuality, your customers are searching for a "foot doctor." You may refer to your product as a "cost-effective doohickey" but your potential customers are looking for a "cheap doohickey." Think about how your customers would best describe your company, product or service and listen for the phrases that they are most likely to use.

Handy Keyword Research Tools & Links:

www.Adwords.Google.com/select/KeywordToolExternal

www.Google Trends

www.KeywordMixer.com

www.Tinyurl.com/typomaker - 20% of all google searches are misspelled which translates to cheap pay-per-click traffic for you!

Maximizing Your Key(word) Moneymaker

How do you describe your product or service?

_____
_____
_____
_____

What 3 words or phrases describe your product or service?

_____
_____
_____
_____

What words would others use to describe your product or service?

_____
_____
_____
_____

List as many related keywords (and keyword phrases) as you can think of here:

_____
_____
_____
_____
_____
_____
_____
_____

Now use the keyword tools listed to create additional keywords and list them here:

Google Related Search

Coincidentally, there's another powerful tool that instantly taps into hidden streams of cheap, targeted traffic, and virtually eliminates your competition.

It's called Google Related Search and has several useful applications which are based off the idea of mind-mapping.

According to Wikipedia, mind-mapping is 'a diagram used to represent words, ideas, tasks, or other items linked to and arranged around a central keyword or idea. Mind maps are used to generate, visualize, structure and classify ideas and as an aid in study, organization, problem-solving, decision-making and writing.'

Imagine an old-fashioned spoke wheel on Western wagons that were used to transport families. Google once offered a visual version of this feature called the Wonder Wheel. For some strange reason, they decided to retire this extremely useful tool, but we can still use the Related Search tool and gather important intelligence gathering data.

If you find relevant keywords in addition to the words and phrases you'd originally suspected, and what we call 'long tail keywords,' by using this tool you can save money on advertising and actually make more money by targeting the related keywords that you now know people are actually searching for.

This is where it starts to get interesting. You can navigate your way around the relevant keywords and phrases and find more and more results. For example, if I wanted to target potential customers looking for free business card offers, I would quickly see that free business card flyers is also a good keyword phrase to target as well. Each time I click on a related search term I can easily see how many searches are being conducted on this term and determine if, as a Marketer, this is a keyword phrase that I want to actively market to.

This helps my SEO strategies and Adwords campaigns tremendously because I am no longer guessing which search terms people might be using nor am I casting an arbitrary net so wide that I am throwing money and time at a bunch of useless terms just hoping they will be profitable.

Another great way to use this tool is to brainstorm content ideas for your articles, videos or blog posts. Google even lets you sort the results based on how recent the activity was. So if it is a hot topic that is surfacing across the net, this is a great opportunity to incorporate that subject matter into your content and capture some of the traffic.

Just make sure that you have a system in place on your website to turn this valuable traffic into leads by capturing their contact information with an opt-in form and Auto-responder. An auto-responder is a vital part of your email marketing strategy that automatically send pre-scheduled email responses to individuals who sign up for your list.

There are so many types of new media marketing strategies you can choose from:

- Email

- Podcasts

- Internet Video Marketing

- Internet Radio

- Internet Commercials

- Auto-responders
- Pay-per-click Campaigns
- Information Products
- Twitter, Facebook Fan Pages, MySpace, LinkedIn
- Blogging
- YouTube
- Free Downloads
- Forums, Discussion Groups, Message Boards
- Article Marketing
- Newsletters
- Joint Ventures
- And that's just to name a few...

So get started by choosing your primary strategy and mastering it with consistent implementation and continual improvement. The worst sin you can commit is a one-shot marketing effort.

Ringing The Register With Google AdWords

Handy Links:

www.adwords.google.com

Back in the early days of internet marketing infancy, you could buy clicks for a nickel or a dime and easily dominate your keyword niche.

But that is no longer the case. Now that more people are hip to using pay-per-click advertising, the arena has quickly become overcrowded and hyper-competitive.

While your competitors duke it out for the same hyped-up, over-saturated keywords at $10 per click or more, you can sneak in under the radar like a stealth ninja and legally steal their profits!

Although the scope of this book does not cover how to set-up a Google AdWords account or campaign management, there are countless books and articles dedicated to this topic. The most widely read being Perry Marshall's ***Definitive Guide To Google Adwords.*** We will continue focusing on natural search engine rankings. But I would be remiss not to at least mention pay-per-click here. It can definitely be a strong supporter of your overall online marketing strategy.

Google's pay-per-click advertisements are short, consisting of a headline and two additional lines of text. Advertisers *(that's you)* select the keywords that will trigger their ads and the maximum amount they agree to pay per click. When a user searches on Google, ads for relevant words are shown as "sponsored links" on the right side of the screen, and sometimes above the main search results.

The ordering of the paid results depends on other advertisers' bids (PPC) and the "quality score" of all ads shown for a given search. Factors such as quality score are calculated by historical click-through rates, relevance of an advertiser's ad text and keywords, an advertiser's account history, and other factors determined by Google's ever-changing algorithms.

Google also uses their quality score to set the minimum bids for an advertiser's keywords. The minimum bid takes into consideration the quality of the landing page, which includes the relevancy and originality of content, ability to navigate, and transparency into the nature of the business. When SEO struggles to deliver top rankings for competitive phrases, pay-per-click ads can fill in the gap. With pay-per-click advertising, you can also implement image and text based advertising on other related websites that are looking to make additional money from Google.

The Power Of Google Places

Handy Links:

www.youtube.com/googleplaces

Google stated that one of every five searches a user performs on their search engine is related to location. In an effort to make Google more local, in 2010 they launched Google Places. For local businesses, your Places page essentially acts as a mini-site where your location information, website address and contact details are displayed. You can add photos, videos, coupons, hours of operation, products, list of services and real-time updates. It is also a convenient place where customers can post reviews of their interaction with your company. Claiming your Places page gives you a ton of exposure on the world's number one most visited site on the web. A Places page listing receives prominent placement on the first page of search results so it is extremely important that you claim and optimize your page right away.

Some additional key elements affect your search engine placement on Google:

1. Take the time to fill out those forms and get yourself listed in the local directories. Don't Delay!

2. When people take the time to do this, it creates more exposure and higher visibility in search engines. If you've got customers or clients who are raving fans and they tell you how much they love what you do, ask them to take a few minutes to write a review for your business. And now, we have the Google Plus feature which broadcasts how many of your friends 'like' the things you're browsing on the web. It's like an informal vote of approval. Encourage this by placing a Google +1 box, social media or Yelp link with a call-to-action on the front page of your site and in the contact us or comments section on your website.

Every dollar counts to local businesses. Claim your listing on free online directories. Make sure that your information is consistent across all of the directories. Your online profile will carry more weight and reinforce memorability if it is consistent across the internet and it will avoid confusion as well.

The key with this strategy is to be sure to include the same information on each one of the directories you submit to including Google Places. Google's spiders crawl the web and cross-reference your listings to check for consistency. Fill in the blanks here and keep it handy to ensure that your online profiles stay consistent:

Company Name:

_____

Telephone Number:

_____

Website URL:

_____

Physical Address:

_____
_____
_____

Description of Services being sure to include your keywords in your description:

_____
_____
_____
_____
_____
_____

List of top 10 images you will use already optimized for your keywords:

_____
_____
_____
_____
_____

Optimizing Your Images

Another important tip we should cover has to do with on-site SEO. This is optimization which involves the HTML code running behind the scenes on your website. Make sure that before you upload an image that you name it with relevant keywords for your pages and that you use the 'alt' attribute – you can make them the same as your image name when adding your code.

Although it might not be as powerful as other techniques, every effort adds up and is a good habit to adopt when using images. Google images search can also bring you a boost of added traffic by using this technique.

Image Naming – Use descriptive file names for your images and make sure your keywords are included. Use hyphens (-) as the separator instead of underscores(_) for file names more than one word. If you have an image of a red cowboy boot on your ecommerce site it is always better to name it as Red-Cowboy-Boot-For-Sale.jpg, rather than using a default name like IMG002938.jpg or even just Boots.jpg

Alt Attributes – Again, always use a suitable descriptive alt attribute with your keywords in them. Alt attributes are the prime source of reference for search engines to understand an image and inform the reader when images won't load or are turned off. Make sure your alt attribute describes your image properly. Since a search engine is not an actual person and can not see what image is showing, the alt attribute is what tells the search engine what the image represents.

Title for Image – Include your keywords in the Title tags on your webpage as well.

Header Tags – When you place a headline or title in a header tag, this signals to the search engines that a particular word or phrase is important and extremely relevant. As a result, the search engines give more weight to words placed in header tags so be sure to include your keywords here.

These strategies involve editing the HTML code of your website and may be beyond your level of interest or expertise. If that is the case, just make sure that any designer or webmaster you hire is performing these routine practices to give your website the most exposure possible.

Online Directories

Search engines like Google, Bing and Yahoo have their own directories that are heavily reliant on keyword terms and there are many other types of directories. Internet listing directories such as Yelp, Yellow Pages, Yellow Book and Super Pages have free, as well as, paid listings. Yellow Page type listings also use your IP address as proof of location, which is a numerical electronic address linked to your computer.

Make sure you register your business name with all of the free directories first. Then you can decide if you want to pursue paid listings. A quick Google search will give you the directories that specialize in your particular industry. Increase visibility for you and you local business by registering with these providers.

Register your business with ALL of the online directories, even if your website is not up yet (or finished). You can then upload pictures of your product to Flickr or on your Facebook fan page and use this link until your website is up. Some of the major listings include:

GetListed.org

SubmitExpress.com

AskCity.com

Bing: https://ssl.bing.com/listings/ListingCenter.aspx

BrownBook.net

BusinessDirectory.bizjournals.com

CityGuide.com

Citysearch.com

CitySlick.net

CitySquares.com

DexKnows.com

InsiderPages.com

Kudzu.com

Local.com

Local.botw.org

LocalAdlink.com

LocalDatabase.com

Google Places: Google.com/places

Matchpoint.com

Merchantcircle.com

Openlist.com

Sitejabber.com

Superpages.com

Switchboard.com

Yahoo! Search: listings.local.yahoo.com

Yelp! yelp.com

Yellowbook.com

Yellowpages.com

Zagat.com

Since the web is constantly changing, some of these links may change as well. If you stumble across a link that's no longer active, simply perform an internet search for that name to find its new website link.

Using Article Directories And Press Releases To Increase Search Rankings

Handy Links:

www.ezinearticles.com
www.articledashboard.com
www.goarticles.com

Did you know there is a way to get extremely targeted website traffic by writing tips for your target audience?

An effective way to get natural (organic) search engine placement at no cost is by targeting key phrases within articles you write that have low competing pages in Google. Seek out a keyword that receives a search volume of at least 1000 per month plus have few competing pages on Google. Search results of 500,000 competition is okay, under 100,000 is ideal, but results beneath 40,000 or fewer competition indicates a keyword or phrase that will be relatively easy to rank for using these techniques and you will quickly show up on the first page.

However, there is a trick to achieving high natural search engine optimization rankings. Whenever you submit your article to multiple article submission websites, make certain that your article content is unique. If it is not, you will be penalized by a duplicate content material penalty and your rankings will suffer.

Also a good practice is to publish your article on your blog first so that your website receives full credit as the article originator, as opposed to publishing it first on Ezine articles who would then receive the bulk of the search engine juice and backlinks.

Write articles of interest to your target audience and post them to article directories including Articlebase, Ezine Articles, ArticleCity and Idea Marketers. Or you can simply do a search for "article directories" and pick the most popular ones to submit your articles. Ezine gets ranked well in the organic search engine results so if you target your keywords and have a catchy title that attracts attention, that is another low-cost traffic and lead generation source for you.

You can also post ads on Craigslist. The cool thing about Craigslist is that it accepts HTML mark-up language which means that you can include live hyperlinks to your images and text that will drive traffic back to your site. Craigslist ads run for seven days but you are allowed to repost your listings without the need to recreate them from scratch. You can create it one time and repost it indefinitely to generate on-going traffic back to your website.

Be sure that your target key phrases are referenced several times throughout the article, especially the beginning and also the end, to realize the very best results from a natural search. Also use the bio box provided at the bottom of every article to include a call-to-action with your website address. This means that you should give readers a compelling reason to click over to your website for additional information.

Promoting Your Product With Online Video

What if you could measure the return on your marketing and advertising dollars, knowing exactly which strategies are performing for you?

Well, there is a strategy that is currently outperforming all avenues of traditional marketing. It's working like gangbusters all over the Internet right now. If you have been hanging anywhere around the World Wide Web lately, you may have noticed a convergence of trends. The main one being video on the Web.

Video marketing is the hottest marketing medium right now with a steady upward trend predicted to last for the next few years. Savvy marketers and small business owners are using it to become main-street internet celebrities in their local areas. A cleverly constructed video marketing campaign can easily outperform all of the traditional advertising you've been doing. It leverages the power of the internet to generate instant exposure and qualified leads for your business. Video gives you more powerful results for less than the cost of just one of the ads you will place on the radio, television or Yellow Pages.

The fact is, when people are looking for a solution to their problem, they hop on the World Wide Web to search for an answer. If you are smart enough to position yourself in front of them exactly when they are looking and provide an answer to their problem, then you become the expert. And guess who they want to buy their solution from? You guessed it...the expert.

	Internet Video	Television Commercials	Newspaper / Magazine Ads	Radio Spots	Billboards	Yellow Pages Ads
Costs	$	$$$	$$$	$$$	$$$	$$
Long Lead Time	X	✓	X	✓	✓	X
Do-It-Yourself	✓	X	X	X	X	X
Laser Focused Targeting	✓	X	X	X	X	X
Measurable Results	✓	X	✓	X	X	✓
Immediate Response	✓	X	X	✓*	X	X
Lasting Exposure	✓	X	X	X	X	✓
Instant Purchase Potential	✓	X	X	✓*	X	X

*With using an 800 number.

Granted there are lots of ways to gain valuable 'face-time' in front of your online prospect. There is Pay-Per-Click, banner ads, search engine optimization, social media and article marketing to name a few. They each have their pros and cons, each sacrificing significant amounts of time and money, or both. But nothing performs better for organic search engine results (as opposed to paid listings) than video.

If you perform a Google search, you will notice the Video search sort button in the upper left corner. YouTube accounts for one-quarter of all Google search traffic in the United States. At the time of this writing, it is the #3 most visited website on the web and increasingly being used as a search engine all its own. That is very powerful information for business owners and marketers.

> **Okay so now let's do the math...**
>
> **6.7 BILLION** Internet Users x 25% on YouTube
> = 16,750,000 **Reasons You Should Be Doing**
>
> **VIDEO MARKETING!**

This means that it is very likely your prospects are already on YouTube searching for videos related to the products and services you offer. Even if your most probable purchasers aren't searching on YouTube for videos related to your product or service, YouTube is owned by Google and gets indexed (i.e. the web crawlers seek out new content and adds the keywords found on it to their directories) more frequently than regular websites. That means that your YouTube video will show up on the Google search results in no time flat! And if you optimize your videos properly, more website traffic, more eager-to-buy prospects and more sales are sure to follow.

The truth is that people do business with folks they Know, Like and Trust. And there is no better way to establish that connection than with online video.

The web is so powerful because it provides a whole world of information at your fingertips. Whether it is a student looking for the nearest late-night fast food joint, or a local florist highlighting this season's wedding favorites, the web has the instantaneous ability to connect you with the information you want right now.

According to the Pew Internet & American Life Project, 72% of Americans were online at least once a day, and 71% of those folks have made online purchases.

The number of individuals who watch retail videos online has grown 40% in the past year. In fact, 82.1 million viewers watched 4.1 billion videos on YouTube which is about 49.8 videos per person. Users also spend fifty-three seconds longer on advertising which contains video. As a side note, the average online video is about 2.8 minutes long, after that, interest fades and a viewer usually clicks away. So keep that in mind when you are creating *your* video marketing campaigns.

Online video marketing also provides a great benefit to you, in that it:

- ✓ Smoothes the buying process
- ✓ Establishes a level of trust with your prospects quickly
- ✓ Saves on gas, travel time and the initial learning curve about your product/service
- ✓ Reduces repetitive conversations
- ✓ Helps to explain complex ideas

Forrester Research reports that adding a simple three minute video into an email increases click-thru rates by 2-3 times!

That creates an exciting opportunity for small business owners and entrepreneurs to reach new and existing customers in increasingly cost-effective ways by laser-targeting their marketing efforts. If your customers are online, doesn't it make sense that you would join them there?

But it is not as simple as slapping your :30 sec television commercial spot on the internet and expecting customers to come flying through the doors to buy from you. The Internet caters to a completely different mindset and you must play by its rules in order to win.

Local internet marketing strategies are a little different from national businesses but they are simple to implement. These strategies are the quickest and most effective way to increasing your overall exposure for your target audience of potential buyers.

Here are just a few of the markets that are benefiting from instant local celebrity status using online video:

- Doctors, Dentists, Plastic Surgeons and other Medical Specialists

- Lawyers

- Certified Public Accountants

- Consultants

- Counseling Agencies/Counselors

- City Municipalities

- Community Colleges

- Personal Fitness Trainers

- Public Service Organizations

- Niche Retail Owners (i.e. Candy Shops, Hardware Stores, Bike Shops, Skating Rinks, Pizza Shops)

- Service Providers (i.e. Plumbers, Electricians, Lawn-care, Music Instructors, Auto Mechanics)

- Book Authors

- Anyone explaining a concept or service

You can finally stop worrying if anyone will walk through your doors today, because by using the strategies covered in this book, you'll attract them like a magnet.

As long as you provide value to your customer base and keep their needs in the forefront, you will continue to be rewarded with on-going business and referrals.

The truth is, the internet is turning into one big cat-fight for today's Marketer. And if you are in any type of business, then you are a Marketer so get used to the idea. Those who market the best and most cost-efficiently, win. Hands down.

6 Secrets To Creating Your Online Video Sales Magnet:

1) Create a YouTube Channel for your business.

2) Include keyword phrase(s) in your video title and in your video description.

3) Create an engaging video. It should be funny, entertaining or provide valuable information to your target audience. How-to videos are extremely popular and demonstrate your expertise while avoiding a hard-sell.

4) Brand your video by including your website info and hyperlinks.

5) Include a Call-To-Action. We discussed this in earlier chapters and the same is true for your videos. You want to give the viewer a compelling reason to click through to your website

and take a desired action. Tell them exactly what you want them to do next.

6) Use high quality visuals and sound.

To see examples of successful company branded YouTube channels that have received enormous exposure, visit YouTube and type "will it blend?" or "orabrush" in the search bar. Watch closely how these companies have used the six secrets in their video marketing and start implementing these strategies in your online videos today.

Google Trends

Handy Links:

www.google.com/trends

Now if you are not familiar with **Google Trends**, this is yet another fabulous tool for savvy business owners to have in their marketing arsenal. Google Trends lets you compare the world's interest in your favorite topics. Enter up to five topics in the search field and see how often they have been searched on Google over time. This search is different from the regular search bar you are used to seeing and shows monthly search volume. Google Trends also shows how frequently your topics have appeared in Google News stories, and in which geographic regions people have searched for them most.

Hot Topics is yet another feature and allows you to see a snapshot of what people are saying, by viewing the topics with the most buzz in recent news, on Twitter, FriendFeed, or other similar sources. **Hot Searches**, on the other hand, shows you a snapshot of what is on the collective mind by viewing the fastest-rising searches over a specific time period. You can see a list of today's top 40 fastest-rising search queries in the U.S. You can also select a recent date in history to see what the top rising searches were and what the search activity looked like over the course of that day. All valuable information for a smart marketer. or business owner

Other Search Tools:

- Google Keyword tool

- Google Related Search

- Google Alerts

How To Avoid Online Overwhelm

Do not worry about becoming overwhelmed with all of the new media marketing necessary to boost your business. You do not have to implement all of the strategies we covered. And certainly not all at once. But hopefully you have taken note of a few that resonated with you. You can implement them over time. Work your way through all of the strategies using this workbook as your guide. Refer back to it often as you master one strategy and then proceed to layer in another.

The most important thing is to simply take action. You can listen, watch or read this information and get fired up with fresh new ideas to grow your business, but if you do not take action and do something, it will be all for naught. Do not sit on this information! Everyday that you delay could cost your business thousands of dollars.

So whatever you do, just do something. Take inspired action because every step builds upon itself and before you know it, you have a complete online marketing strategy that will generate leads for your business even while you sleep.

Every penny is precious to the lifeblood of your business. You know that you need to market and advertise your products & services in order to keep a steady stream of leads and prospects. But somehow the money you're spending on advertising just isn't bringing quality leads in the door and you are not sure why or how to fix the leak and fill your sales funnel.

Besides, who has the time? There are so many tasks on your "To Do" list that marketing your business always gets pushed to the back-burner or addressed intermittently without focus or consistency.

If you're guilty of only marketing when business slows down, that's no way to maintain consistent sales. We understand that in between doing all the multi tasking yourself, you might not have the time to promote your business through the latest new media tactics available to you.

It could be possible that your customers may miss your promotional activities on television, radio, or even internet but it is rare they will miss it on their cell phone. You can provide your customers with various benefits and at the same time promote your business.

FAST FACTS On Mobile Websites:

- One-half of all Internet searches for LOCAL products and services are performed from mobile devices.

- Approximately 96 million mobile searches performed in 2009 were by those looking for a "location–based" (i.e.

local) service. This number is expected to grow to more than 526 million searches by 2012.

- Traditional websites are designed to be viewed on a computer screen instead of a mobile device. This means that most regular websites are not compatible with mobile devices. Is yours?

- Mobile-friendly websites receive higher mobile search engine rankings. This means that when people search for your type of product or service using their mobile device, you can show up higher in the results just because you have a mobile website.

- Easier for "on the go" visitors to find your business and contact you with one-click calling, one-click email, and instant directions. This eliminates the need for your customers to take "extra steps" in order to contact or visit your business.

- Gives you the advantage over your competitors; most of which are not leveraging the powerful benefits of mobile marketing.

- Integrating social media platforms such as Facebook, Twitter, and YouTube with your mobile website boost your profits even more.

So if you have not considered how you will incorporate mobile websites, mobile marketing and QR codes into your overall marketing strategy, then wouldn't *now* be a perfect time to do so?

Scan the following QR code with your smartphone's camera (you must first download a free QR code reader app) to see how it works. Try it...it's fun and it's free!

My goal is that you use the information here to propel your business forward using these powerful tools. It doesn't serve you if the information simply sits on your desk collecting dust so get out there and start using it!

If you have found value in this material, there are more than a few ways to stay engaged. I invite you to leave a review on the book's Amazon.com page, "Like" Eclectic Design Studio on **Facebook** at *www.Facebook.com/EclecticDesignStudio*, or subscribe to the EclecticDesignStudio channel on **YouTube** at *www.YouTube.com/EclecticDesignStudio* to stay connected and also see these marketing strategies in action.

To Your Success!

Internet Terms Decoded

Being a player in the online game takes skill and dedication. By familiarizing yourself with some of the common terms you will lay a solid foundation for success in this competitive arena, sound more knowledgeable to your web designer and get maximum results from your online efforts. Here's an abbreviated list to get you started...

Adsense - Code from Google that you put on your site which allows relevant advertisements to show up on your site. You receive money every time someone clicks on the ads that subsequently appear on your site.

Adwords - Google's PPC program, also MSN/Bing and Yahoo! and other search engines where your ad appears in search results based on the keywords you specify. You pay a certain amount for each click you receive as a result of the network displaying your ad. Prices vary depending on the competitiveness of the keyword and how well your ads perform (the higher the click-through rate, the less you pay per click).

Anchor text - The blue text on a hyperlink. Search engines use the anchor text that websites assign to the hyperlink as an indicator of what your page is really about.

Article Marketing - Writing and submitting articles to directories in order to get traffic to your site.

Auto-responder - A service that provides an automated stream of emails to people who have signed up on your list.

Bio box - The area at the bottom of an article where you can talk about yourself and your services. It is a good traffic generation strategy to use this area to list your site and give people a reason to go visit the site.

Call-To-Action - A sentence or two that tells people specifically what action to take. For example, *"Click Here to Download Your Free Report."*

Continuity Program - A product that has a reoccurring billing feature.

Conversion Rate - The average number of people who purchase your offer for every 100 visitors or clicks your site receives.

CTR - Click-through-rate, the average number of people who click on your advertisement for every 100 impressions it receives.

Double Opt-in - When you have to confirm that you have indeed signed-up for a particular email list. This is usually done by clicking on a link in a confirmation email you receive shortly after submitting your email address to a particular site. Helps to avoid spam and unintentional email submits.

Downsell - Offering a cheaper alternative to an offer if someone visits the order page and leaves without making a purchase.

Ezine - Digital newsletter delivered via email.

External links - (a.k.a. Backlinks) Links to your website from other websites.

Forced Continuity - Usually offered as a limited time "free trial," forced continuity is when you are automatically entered into a continuity after the initial test drive period has expired.

FTP - File Transfer Protocol, the protocol used to transfer your website files to the server that hosts your site.

HTML - The main language that websites are written in.

IP Address - A string of numbers that is used to locate devices connected to the internet. Every website/computer has a corresponding numerical address.

Keyword/Keyword Phrase - A word or group of words that people enter into a search engine like Google, Yahoo! and Bing in order to research information on a particular topic.

Niche - A particular subset of any market.

Opt-in - When someone gives you their contact information via a submission form on your website or social media profiles, giving you permission to contact them again via email.

Outsourcing - Hiring temporary workers or companies to complete work on your behalf.

PPC - Pay Per Click, advertisements that you put on display in which you only pay if someone clicks on your ad and visits your site.

Reciprocal links - Linking to a website in exchange for their site linking back to yours.

ROI - Return on investment, how much income you make from a project or advertisement compared to the amount you spent to launch and manage it.

SEO - The strategies and tactics used to maximize your online exposure in the organic search results for keywords you target. The goal is to appear in the top spots of the organic search engine results for your targeted keywords.

Spam - Unsolicited email messages.

BONUS MATERIAL!

Try Google AdWords For Free

Visit this link and receive $75 to try your first pay-per-click campaign:

www.EclecticDesignStudio.net/freegoogle

Order "Search Engine Success for Newbies" for your organization or association!

Search Engine Success is a great resource to arm entrepreneurs, small business owners and independent professionals with the knowledge and action steps necessary to succeed online. Order today and share these sales success strategies with those in your circles of influence who are ready to take action but need help with all-important that first step.

IMPORTANT NOTICE: Please allow 7-14 business days for shipping. *Bulk orders are non-returnable. Be sure to verify the product indicated and quantity requested are correct, and ensure that you have read the Terms & Conditions at the bottom of the order form prior to faxing your order to the bulk-order department.*

THIS FORM MAY ONLY BE USED FOR 50 OR MORE COPIES GOING TO ONE LOCATION. To order less than 50 copies, please visit Amazon.com so that your order can be fulfilled in the most timely & efficient manner possible.

Please mail/fax/email your order to:
Eclectic Design Studio
7601 W. 185th Street
Tinley Park, IL 60477
Tel: (888) 857-5756
Fax: (404) 953-6965
Email: info@eclecticdesignstudio.net

STEP 1 — Order Your Items

TODAYS DATE: _____

Quantity Discounts: 50 - 99 units | 100 - 999 units | 1000 + units
Special Unit Price: $11.07 each | $10.37 each | $9.17 each

TITLE	QUANTITY	UNIT PRICE	COST
(Paperback Book) **Search Engine Success for Newbies:** *How Your Local Business Can Skyrocket Sales Using FREE Online Advertising*			
(Audio CD) **Search Engine Success for Newbies:** *How Your Local Business Can Skyrocket Sales Using FREE Online Advertising*			
		Shipping	
		Subtotal	
		Tax 8.50%	
		Total $	

STEP 2 — Enter Contact Info

SHIPPING INFORMATION:

Name: _____
Street Address: _____
City: _____
State: _____ **Zip:** _____
Telephone #: _____

BILLING INFORMATION:

Payment Type: ❏ Visa ❏ Mastercard ❏ Discover
❏ American Express ❏ Check

Name on Card: _____

Card Billing Address: ❏ *(Check if same as shipping)*

_____

Card Number: _____
Exp. Date: _____ **CVC Code:** _____
Cardholder's Telephone: _____
Cardholder's Email: _____

(this will be used for all communication regarding this order.)

Tax Exempt? ❏ Yes ❏ No *(Please provide certificate number and submit a copy of the certificate with your order form)*

STEP 3 — Select Shipping Method

❏ **Standard Ground** (10 to 15 business days) **Cost:** $9.95
❏ **2nd Day** (3 to 5 business days) **Cost:** Additional $7.49 per order fee
❏ **Next Day** (1 to 3 business days) **Cost:** Additional $12.49 per order fee
❏ **International and Canadian Express** (1 to 7 business days) **Cost:** Additional $29.99 per order fee

TERMS & CONDITIONS:

• <u>*Bulk orders are non-returnable.*</u> *Should there be an event where a return is approved; the return is subject to a $3 per item restocking fee less shipping fees.*

Inventory is subject to change. Your quote is valid for 10 business days. If a price quote is accepted after 10 business days, you will receive an updated price quote for your approval prior to proceeding.

International Shipment (outside of the contiguous United States) Charges are based on weight and destination. In accordance with applicable law, Eclectic Design Studio collects tax in all states. Sales tax is applied to the total amount of the order and is based on the shipment's destination state and local sales tax rates. Goods and Services Tax (GST) applicable when shipping to Canada.

If you have any additional questions or comments, please email us at <u>info@eclecticdesignstudio.net</u> or if you prefer, you may call a Business Solutions Representative at 888-857-5756.

Thank You For Your Order!

Made in the USA
Monee, IL
19 February 2022